# lord
# byron

## selected poems

SWEET WATER PRESS

*lord byron*
*selected poems*

Produced by Cliff Road Books

ISBN: 1-58173-499-9
ISBN-13: 978-1-58173-499-7

Design by Pat Covert

Printed in China

# Table of Contents

# lord
# byron

selected poems

# To Caroline

Think'st thou I saw thy beauteous eyes,
    Suffused in tears, implore to stay;
And heard unmoved thy plenteous sighs,
    Which said far more than words can say?

Though keen the grief thy tears exprest,
    When love and hope lay both o'erthrown;
Yet still, my girl, this bleeding breast
    Throbb'd with deep sorrow as thine own.

But when our cheeks with anguish glow'd,
    When thy sweet lips were join'd to mine,
The tears that from my eyelids flow'd
    Were lost in those which fell from thine.

Thou couldst not feel my burning cheek,
    Thy gushing tears had quench'd its flame;
And as thy tongue essay'd to speak,
    In sighs alone it breathed my name.

And yet, my girl, we weep in vain,
    In vain our fate in sighs deplore;
Remembrance only can remain,—
    But that will make us weep the more.

Again, thou best beloved, adieu!
    Ah! if thou canst, o'ercome regret;
Nor let thy mind past joys review,—
    Our only hope is to forget!

## To a Beautiful Quaker

Sweet girl! though only once we met,
That meeting I shall ne'er forget;
And though we ne'er may meet again,
Rememberance will thy form retain.
I would not say, "I love," but still
My senses struggle with my will:
In vain, to drive thee from my breast,
My thoughts are more and more represt;
In vain I check the rising sighs,
Another to the last replies:
Perhaps this is not love, but yet
Our meeting I can ne'er forget.

What though we never silence broke,
Our eyes a sweeter language spoke.
The tongue in flattering falsehood deals,
And tells a tale it never feels;
Deceit the guilty lips impart,
And hush the mandates of the heart;
But soul's interpreters, the eyes,
Spurn such restraint and scorn disguise.
As thus our glances oft conversed,
And all our bosoms felt, rehearsed,
No spirit, from within, reproved us,
Say rather, "'twas the spirit moved us."
Though what they utter'd I repress,
Yet I conceive thou'lt partly guess;
For as on thee my memory ponders,

Perchance to me thine also wanders,
This for myself, at least, I'll say,
Thy form appears through night, through day:
Awake, with it my fancy teems;
In sleep, it smiles in fleeting dreams;
The vision charms the hours away,
And bids me curse Aurora's ray
For breaking slumbers of delight
Which make me wish for endless night:
Since, oh! whate'er my future fate,
Shall joy or woe my steps await,
Tempted by love, by storms beset,
Thine image I can ne'er forget.

Alas! again no more we meet,
No more our former looks repeat;
Then let me breathe this parting prayer,
The dictate of my bosom's care:
"May Heaven so guard my lovely quaker,
That anguish never can o'ertake her;
That peace and virture ne'er forsake her,
But bliss be aye her heart's partaker!
Oh, may the happy mortal, fated
To be by dearest ties related,
For her each hour new joys discover,
And lose the husband in the lover!
May that fair bosom never know
What 'tis to feel the restless woe
Which stings the soul with vain regret,
Of him who never can forget!"

## To Eliza

### 1

Eliza! what fools are the Mussulman sect,
  Who, to woman, deny the soul's future existence;
Could they see thee, Eliza! they'd own their defect,
  And this doctrine would meet with a general
    resistance.

### 2

Had their prophet possess'd half an atom of sense,
  He ne'er would have *woman* from Paradise driven;
Instead of his *Houris*, a flimsy pretence,
  With *woman alone* he had peopled his Heaven.

### 3

Yet, still, to increase your calamities more,
  Not content with depriving your bodies of spirit,
He allots one poor husband to share amongst
    four!—
  With *souls* you'd dispense; but, this last, who
    could bear it?

### 4

His religion to please neither *party* is made;
  On *husbands* 'tis *hard*, to the wives most uncivil;
Still I can't contradict, what so oft has been said,
  "Though women are angels, yet wedlock's the
    devil."

### 5

This terrible truth, even Scripture has told,
    Ye Benedicks! hear me, and listen with rapture;
If a glimpse of redemption you wish to behold,
    Of St. Matt.—read the second and twentieth
        chapter.


### 6

'Tis surely enough upon earth to be vex'd,
    With wives who eternal confusion are spreading;
"But in Heaven," (so runs the Evangelist's Text,)
    "We neither have giving in marriage, or
        wedding."


### 7

From this we suppose, (as indeed well we may,)
    That should Saints after death, with their
        spouses put up more,
And wives, as in life, aim at absolute sway,
    All Heaven would ring with the conjugal uproar.


### 8

Distraction and Discord would follow in course,
    Nor Matthew, nor Mark, nor St. Paul, can
        deny it,
The only expedient is general divorce,
    To prevent universal disturbance and riot.

### 9

But though husband and wife shall at length be
　　disjoin'd,
　Yet woman and man ne'er were meant to
　　dissever,
Our chains once dissolv'd, and our hearts
　　unconfin'd,
　We'll love without bonds, but we'll love you
　　forever.

### 10

Though souls are denied you by fools and by
　　rakes,
　Should you own it yourselves, I would even
　　then doubt you,
Your nature so much of *celestial* partakes,
　The Garden of Eden would wither without you.

# Reply to Some Verses of J.M.B. Pigot, Esq.

### 1

Why, Pigot, complain
Of this damsel's disdain,
Why thus in despair do you fret?
For months you may try,
Yet, believe me, a *sigh*
Will never obtain a *coquette*.

### 2

Would you teach her to love?
For a time seem to rove;
At first she may *frown* in a *pet*;
But leave her awhile,
She shortly will smile,
And then you may *kiss* your *coquette*.

### 3

For such are the airs
Of these fanciful fairs,
They think all our *homage* a *debt*:
Yet a partial neglect
Soon takes an effect,
And humbles the proudest *coquette*.

### 4

Dissemble your pain,
And lengthen your chain,
And seem her *hauteur* to *regret*;
If again you shall sigh,
She no more will deny,
That *yours* is the rosy *coquette*.

### 5

If still, from false pride,
Your pangs she deride,
This whimsical virgin forget;
Some *other* admire,
Who will *melt* with your *fire*,
And laugh at the *little coquette*.

### 6

For *me*, I adore
Some *twenty* or more,
And love them most dearly; but yet,
Though my heart they enthral,
I'd abandon them all,
Did they act like your blooming *coquette*.

### 7

No longer repine,
Adopt this design,
And break through her slight-woven net!
Away with despair,
No longer forbear
To fly from the captious *coquette*.

### 8

Then quit her, my friend!
Your bosom defend,
Ere quite with her snares you're beset:
Lest your deep-wounded heart,
When incens'd by the smart
Should lead you to *curse* the *coquette*.

## To M. S. G.

Whene'er I view those lips of thine,
  Their hue invites my fervent kiss;
Yet I forego that bliss divine,
  Alas, it were unhallow'd bliss!

Whene'er I dream of that pure breast,
  How could I dwell upon its snows!
Yet is the daring wish repress'd,
  For that—would banish its repose.

A glance from thy soul-searching eye
  Can raise with hope, depress with fear;
Yet I conceal my love—and why?
  I would not force a painful tear.

I ne'er have told my love, yet thou
  Hast seen my ardent flame too well;
And shall I plead my passion now,
  To make thy bosom's heaven a hell?

No! for thou never canst be mine,
  United by the priest's decree:
By any ties but those divine,
  Mine, my beloved, thou ne'er shalt be.

Then let the secret fire consume,
  Let it consume, thou shalt not know:
With joy I court a certain doom,
  Rather than spread its guilty glow.

I will not ease my tortured heart,
  By driving dove-eyed peace from thine;
Rather than such a sting impart,
  Each thought presumptuous I resign.

Yes! yield those lips, for which I'd brave
  More than I here shall dare to tell;
Thy innocence and mine to save,—
  I bid thee now a last farewell.

Yes! yield that breast, to see despair,
  And hope no more thy soft embrace;
Which to obtain my soul would dare,
  All, all reproach—but thy disgrace.

At least from guilt shalt thou be free,
  No matron shall thy shame reprove;
Though cureless pangs may prey on me,
  No martyr shalt thou be to love.

# The First Kiss of Love

Α βαρβιτος  δε χορδαις
Ερωτα μουνον  ηχει.
—ANACREON

### 1

Away with your fictions of flimsy romance,
  Those tissues of falsehood which Folly has wove;
Give me the mild beam of the soul-breathing glance,
  Or the rapture which dwells on the first kiss of
      love.

### 2

Ye rhymers, whose bosoms with fantasy glow,
  Whose pastoral passions are made for the grove;
From what blest inspiration your sonnets would
      flow,
  Could you ever have tasted the first kiss of love!

### 3

If Apollo should e'er his assistance refuse,
  Or the Nine be dispos'd from your service to rove,
Invoke them no more, bid adieu to the Muse,
  And try the effect, of the first kiss of love.

### 4

I hate you, ye cold compositions of art,
  Though prudes may condemn me, and bigots
      reprove;

20

I court the effusions that spring from the heart,
   Which throbs, with delight, to the first kiss of
      love.


5

Your shepherds, your flocks, those fantastical
      themes,
   Perhaps may amuse, yet they never can move:
Arcadia displays but a region of dreams;
   What are visions like these, to the first kiss of
      love?


6

Oh! cease to affirm that man, since his birth,
   From Adam, till now, has with wretchedness
      strove;
Some portion of Paradise still is on earth,
   And Eden revives, in the first kiss of love.


7

When age chills the blood, when our pleasures are
      past—
   For years fleet away with the wings of the
      dove—
The dearest remembrance will still be the last,
   Our sweetest memorial, the first kiss of love.

## L'amitié, Est L'amour Sans Ailes

### 1

Why should my anxious breast repine,
  Because my youth is fled?
Days of delight may still be mine;
  Affection is not dead.
In tracing back the years of youth,
One firm record, one lasting truth
  Celestial consolation brings;
Bear it, ye breezes, to the seat,
Where first my heart responsive beat,—
  "Friendship is Love without his wings!"

### 2

Through few, but deeply chequer'd years,
  What moments have been mine!
Now half obscured by clouds of tears,
  Now bright in rays divine;
Howe'er my future doom be cast,
My soul, enraptur'd with the past,
  To one idea fondly clings;
Friendship! that thought is all thine own,
Worth worlds of bliss, that thought alone—
  "Friendship is Love without his wings!"

### 3

Where yonder yew-trees lightly wave
  Their branches on the gale,
Unheeded heaves a simple grave,

Which tells the common tale;
Round this unconscious schoolboys stray,
Till the dull knell of childish play
    From yonder studious mansion rings;
But here, whene'er my footsteps move,
My silent tears too plainly prove,
    "Friendship is Love without his wings!"

4

Oh, Love, before thy glowing shrine,
    My early vows were paid;
My hopes, my dreams, my heart was thine,
    But these are now decay'd;
For thine are pinions like the wind,
No trace of thee remains behind,
    Except, alas! thy jealous stings.
Away, away! delusive power,
Thou shall not haunt my coming hour;
    Unless, indeed, without thy wings.

5

Seat of my youth! thy distant spire
    Recalls each scene of joy;
My bosom glows with former fire,—
    In mind again a boy.
Thy grove of elms, thy verdant hill,
Thy every path delights me still,
    Each flower a double fragrance flings;
Again, as once, in converse gay,
Each dear associate seems to say,
    "Friendship is Love without his wings!'

### 6

My Lycus! wherefore dost thou weep?
  Thy falling tears restrain;
Affection for a time may sleep,
  But, oh, 'twill wake again.
Think, think, my friend, when next we meet,
Our long-wish'd interview, how sweet!
  From this my hope of rapture springs;
While youthful hearts thus fondly swell,
Absence, my friend, can only tell,
  "Friendship is Love without his wings!"

### 7

In one, and one alone deceiv'd,
  Did I my error mourn?
No—from oppressive bonds reliev'd,
  I left the wretch to scorn.
I turn'd to those my childhood knew,
With feelings warm, with bosoms true,
  Twin'd with my heart's according strings;
And till those vital chords shall break,
For none but these my breast shall wake
  Friendship, the power deprived of wings!

### 8

Ye few! my soul, my life is yours,
  My memory and my hope;
Your worth a lasting love insures,
  Unfetter'd in its scope;
From smooth deceit and terror sprung,

With aspect fair and honey'd tongue,
   Let Adulation wait on kings;
With joy elate, by snares beset,
We, we, my friends, can ne'er forget,
   "Friendship is Love without his wings!"


                    9
Fictions and dreams inspire the bard,
   Who rolls the epic song;
Friendship and truth be my reward—
   To me no bays belong;
If laurell'd Fame but dwells with lies,
Me the Enchantress ever flies,
   Whose heart and not whose fancy sings;
Simple and young, I dare not feign;
Mine be the rude yet heartfelt strain,
   "Friendship is Love without his wings!"

# Lachin Y Gair

### 1

Away, ye gay landscapes, ye garden of roses!
    In you let the minions of luxury rove;
Restore me the rocks, where the snow-flake reposes,
    Though still they are sacred to freedom and love:
Yet, Caledonia, belov'd are thy mountains,
    Round their white summits though elements war;
Though cataracts foam 'stead of smooth-flowing
            fountains,
    I sigh for the valley of dark Loch na Garr.

### 2

Ah! there my young footsteps in infancy wander'd;
    My cap was the bonnet, my cloak was the plaid;
On chieftains, long perish'd, my memory ponder'd,
    As daily I strode through the pine-cover'd glade;
I sought not my home, till the day's dying glory
    Gave place to the rays of the bright polar star;
For fancy was cheer'd by traditional story,
    Disclos'd by the natives of dark Loch na Garr.

### 3

"Shades of the dead! have I not heard your voices
    Rise on the night-rolling breath of the gale?"
Surely, the soul of the hero rejoices,
    And rides on the wind, o'er his own Highland
            vale!
Round Loch na Garr, while the stormy mist  gathers,

Winter presides in his cold icy car:
Clouds, there, encircle the forms of my Fathers;
    They dwell in the tempests of dark Loch na Garr.

4

"Ill-starr'd, though brave, did no visions foreboding
    Tell you that fate had forsaken your cause?"
Ah! were you destin'd to die at Culloden,
    Victory crown'd not your fall with applause:
Still were you happy, in Death's earthy slumber,
    You rest with your clan, in the caves of Braemar;
The Pibroch resounds, to the piper's loud number,
    Your deeds, on the echoes of dark Loch na Garr.

5

Years have roll'd on, Loch na Garr, since I left you,
    Years must elapse, ere I tread you again:
Nature of verdure and flowers has bereft you,
    Yet still are you dearer than Albion's plain:
England! thy beauties are tame and domestic,
    To one who has rov'd on the mountains afar:
Oh! for the crags that are wild and majestic,
    The steep, frowning glories of dark Loch na Garr.

# To Romance

### 1

Parent of golden dreams, Romance!
  Auspicious Queen of childish joys,
Who lead'st along, in airy dance,
  Thy votive train of girls and boys;
At length, in spells no longer bound,
  I break the fetters of my youth;
No more I tread thy mystic round,
  But leave thy realms for those of Truth.

### 2

And yet 'tis hard to quit the dreams
  Which haunt the unsuspicious soul,
Where every nymph a goddess seems,
  Whose eyes through rays immortal roll;
While Fancy holds her boundless reign,
  And all assume a varied hue;
When Virgins seem no longer vain,
  And even Woman's smiles are true.

### 3

And must we own thee, but a name,
  And from thy hall of clouds descend?
Nor find a Sylph in every dame,
  A Pylades in every friend?
But leave, at once, thy realms of air
  To mingling bands of fairy elves;
Confess that woman's false as fair,
  And friends have feeling for—themselves?

### 4

With shame, I own, I've felt thy sway;
  Repentant, now thy reign is o'er;
No more thy precepts I obey,
  No more on fancied pinions soar;
Fond fool! to love a sparkling eye,
  And think that eye to truth was dear;
To trust a passing wanton's sigh,
  And melt beneath a wanton's tear!

### 5

Romance! disgusted with deceit,
  Far from thy motley court I fly,
Where Affection holds her seat,
  And sickly Sensibility;
Whose silly tears can never flow
  For any pangs excepting thine;
Who turns aside from real woe,
  To steep in dew thy gaudy shrine.

### 6

Now join with sable Sympathy,
  With cypress crown'd, array'd in weeds,
Who heaves with thee her simple sigh,
  Whose breast for every bosom bleeds;
And call thy sylvan female choir,
  To mourn a Swain for ever gone,
Who once could glow with equal fire,
  But bends not now before thy throne.

### 7

Ye genial Nymphs, whose ready tears
   On all occasions swiftly flow;
Whose bosoms heave with fancied fears,
   With fancied flames and phrenzy glow;
Say, will you mourn my absent name,
   Apostate from your gentle train?
An infant Bard, at least, may claim
   From you a sympathetic strain.

### 8

Adieu, fond race! a long adieu!
   The hour of fate is hovering nigh;
E'en now the gulf appears in view,
   Where unlamented you must lie:
Oblivion's blackening lake is seen,
   Convuls'd by gales you cannot weather,
Where you, and eke your gentle queen,
   Alas! must perish altogether.

# I Would I Were a Careless Child

### 1

I would I were a careless child,
    Still dwelling in my Highland cave,
Or roaming through the dusky wild,
    Or bounding o'er the dark blue wave;
The cumbrous pomp of Saxon pride,
    Accords not with the freeborn soul,
Which loves the mountain's craggy side,
    And seeks the rocks where billows roll.

### 2

Fortune! take back these cultur'd lands,
    Take back this name of splendid sound!
I hate the touch of servile hands,
    I hate the slaves that cringe around:
Place me among the rocks I love,
    Which sound to Ocean's wildest roar;
I ask but this—again to rove
    Through scenes my youth hath known before.

### 3

Few are my years, and yet I feel
    The World was ne'er design'd for me:
Ah! why do dark'ning shades conceal
    The hour when man must cease to be?
Once I beheld a splendid dream,
    A visionary scene of bliss:
Truth!—wherefore did thy hated beam
    Awake me to a world like this?

### 4

I lov'd—but those I lov'd are gone;
　Had friends—my early friends are fled.
How cheerless feels the heart alone,
　When all its former hopes are dead!
Though gay companions, o'er the bowl
　Dispel awhile the sense of ill;
Though Pleasure stirs the maddening soul,
　The heart—the heart—is lonely still.


### 5

How dull! to hear the voice of those
　Whom Rank or Chance, whom Wealth or Power,
Have made, though neither friends nor foes,
　Associates of the festive hour.
Give me again a faithful few,
　In years and feelings still the same,
And I will fly the midnight crew,
　Where boist'rous Joy is but a name.


### 6

And Woman, lovely Woman! thou,
　My hope, my comforter, my all!
How cold must be my bosom now,
　When e'en thy smiles begin to pall!
Without a sigh would I resign,
　This busy scene of splendid Woe,
To make that calm contentment mine,
　Which Virtue knows, or seems to know.

7

Fain would I fly the haunts of men—
  I seek to shun, not hate mankind;
My breast requires the sullen glen,
  Whose gloom may suit a darken'd mind.
Oh! that to me the wings were given
  Which bear the turtle to her nest!
Then would I cleave the vault of Heaven,
  To flee away, and be at rest.

.

# Farewell! If Ever Fondest Prayer

### 1

Farewell! if ever fondest prayer
  For other's weal availed on high,
Mine will not all be lost in air,
  But waft thy name beyond the sky.
'Twere vain to speak—to weep—to sigh:
  Oh! more than tears of blood can tell,
When wrung from Guilt's expiring eye,
  Are in that word—Farewell!—Farewell!

### 2

These lips are mute, these eyes are dry;
  But in my breast and in my brain,
Awake the pangs that pass not by,
  The thought that ne'er shall sleep again.
My soul nor deigns nor dares complain,
  Though Grief and Passion there rebel:
I only know we loved in vain—
  I only feel—Farewell!—Farewell!

# When We Two Parted

### 1

When we two parted
  In silence and tears,
Half broken-hearted
  To sever for years,
Pale grew thy cheek and cold,
  Colder thy kiss;
Truly that hour foretold
  Sorrow to this.

### 2

The dew of the morning
  Sunk chill on my brow—
It felt like the warning
  Of what I feel now.
Thy vows are all broken,
  And light is thy fame:
I hear thy name spoken,
  And share in its shame.

### 3

They name thee before me,
  A knell to mine ear;
A shudder comes o'er me—
  Why wert thou so dear?
They know not I knew thee,
  Who knew thee too well:—
Long, long shall I rue thee,
  Too deeply to tell.

In secret we met—
  In silence I grieve,
That thy heart could forget,
  Thy spirit deceive.
If I should meet thee
  After long years,
How should I greet thee?—
  With silence and tears.

# There Was A Time, I Need Not Name

There was a time, I need not name,
   Since it will ne'er forgotten be,
When all our feelings were the same
   As still my soul hath been to thee.

And from that hour when first thy tongue
   Confess'd a love which equall'd mine,
Though many a grief my heart hath wrung,
   Unknown and thus unfelt by thine,

None, none hath sunk so deep as this—
   To think how all that love hath flown;
Transient as every faithless kiss,
   But transient in thy breast alone.

And yet my heart some solace knew,
   When late I heard thy lips declare,
In accents once imagined true,
   Remembrance of the days that were.

Yes; my adored, yet most unkind!
   Though thou wilt never love again,
To me 'tis doubly sweet to find
   Remembrance of that love remain.

Yes! 'tis a glorious thought to me,
   Nor longer shall my soul repine,
Whate'er thou art or e'er shalt be,
   Thou hast been dearly, solely mine.

# And Wilt Thou Weep When I Am Low?

### 1

And wilt thou weep when I am low?
  Sweet lady! speak those words again:
Yet if they grieve thee, say not so—
  I would not give that bosom pain.

### 2

My heart is sad, my hopes are gone,
  My blood runs coldly through my breast;
And when I perish, thou alone
  Wilt sigh above my place of rest.

### 3

And yet, methinks, a gleam of peace
  Doth through my cloud of anguish shine:
And for a while my sorrows cease,
  To know thy heart hath felt for mine.

### 4

Oh lady! blessèd be that tear—
  It falls for one who cannot weep;
Such precious drops are doubly dear
  To those whose eyes no tear may steep.

### 5

Sweet lady! once my heart was warm
  With every feeling soft as thine;
But Beauty's self hath ceas'd to charm
  A wretch created to repine.

## 6

Yet wilt thou weep when I am low?
  Sweet lady! speak those words again:
Yet if they grieve thee, say not so—
  I would not give that bosom pain.

# Remind Me Not, Remind Me Not

### 1

Remind me not, remind me not,
  Of those belov'd, those vanish'd hours,
    When all my soul was given to thee;
Hours that may never be forgot,
  Till Time unnerves our vital powers,
    And thou and I shall cease to be.

### 2

Can I forget—canst thou forget,
  When playing with thy golden hair,
    How quick thy fluttering heart did move?
Oh! by my soul, I see thee yet,
  With eyes so languid, breast so fair,
    And lips, though silent, breathing love.

### 3

When thus reclining on my breast,
  Those eyes threw back a glance so sweet,
    As half reproach'd yet rais'd desire,
And still we near and nearer prest,
  And still our glowing lips would meet,
    As if in kisses to expire.

### 4

And then those pensive eyes would close,
  And bid their lids each other seek,
    Veiling the azure orbs below;

While their long lashes' darken'd gloss
　　Seem'd stealing o'er thy brilliant cheek,
　　　Like raven's plumage smooth'd on snow.


5

I dreamt last night our love return'd,
　　And, sooth to say, that very dream
　　　Was sweeter in its phantasy,
Than if for other hearts I burn'd,
　　For eyes that ne'er like thine could beam
　　　In Rapture's wild reality.


6

Then tell me not, remind me not,
　　Of hours which, though for ever gone,
　　　Can still a pleasing dream restore,
Till thou and I shall be forgot,
　　And senseless, as the mouldering stone
　　　Which tells that we shall be no more.

## Lines Inscribed Upon a Cup
## Formed From a Skull

### 1

Start not—nor deem my spirit fled:
   In me behold the only skull,
From which, unlike a living head,
   Whatever flows is never dull.

### 2

I liv'd, I lov'd, I quaff'd, like thee:
   I died: let earth my bones resign;
Fill up—thou canst not injure me;
   The worm hath fouler lips than thine.

### 3

Better to hold the sparkling grape,
   Than nurse the earth-worm's slimy brood;
And circle in the goblet's shape
   The drink of Gods, than reptiles' food.

### 4

Where once my wit, perchance, hath shone,
   In aid of others' let me shine;
And when, alas! our brains are gone,
   What nobler substitute than wine?

### 5

Quaff while thou canst: another race,
   When thou and thine, like me, are sped,

May rescue thee from Earth's embrace,
  And rhyme and revel with the dead.

6

Why not? since through life's little day
  Our heads such sad effects produce;
Redeem'd from worms and wasting clay,
  This chance is theirs, to be of use.

# Inscription on the Monument of a Newfoundland Dog

When some proud son of man returns to earth,
Unknown to glory, but upheld by birth,
The sculptor's art exhausts the pomp of woe
And storied urns record who rest below:
When all is done, upon the tomb is seen,
Not what he was, but what he should have been:
But the poor dog, in life the firmest friend,
The first to welcome, foremost to defend,
Whose honest heart is still his master's own,
Who labours, fights, lives, breathes for him alone,
Unhonour'd falls unnotic'd all his worth—
Denied in heaven the soul he held on earth:
While Man, vain insect! hopes to be forgiven,
And claims himself a sole exclusive Heaven.
Oh Man! thou feeble tenant of an hour,
Debas'd by slavery, or corrupt by power,
Who knows thee well must quit thee with disgust,
Degraded mass of animated dust!
Thy love is lust, thy friendship all a cheat,
Thy smiles hypocrisy, thy words deceit!
By nature vile, ennobled but by name,
Each kindred brute might bid thee blush for shame.
Ye! who perchance behold this simple urn,
Pass on—it honours none you wish to mourn:
To mark a Friend's remains these stones arise;
I never knew but one—and here he lies.

## Stanzas To A Lady,

### 1

'Tis done—and shivering in the gale
The bark unfurls her snowy sail;
And whistling o'er the bending mast,
Loud sings on high the fresh'ning blast;
And I must from this land be gone,
Because I cannot love but one.

### 2

But could I be what I have been,
And could I see what I have seen—
Could I repose upon the breast
Which once my warmest wishes blest—
I should not seek another zone,
Because I cannot love but one.

### 3

'Tis long since I beheld that eye
Which gave me bliss or misery;
And I have striven, but in vain,
Never to think of it again:
For though I fly from Albion,
I still can only love but one.

### 4

As some lone bird, without a mate,
My weary heart is desolate;
I look around, and cannot trace
One friendly smile or welcome face,
And ev'n in crowds am still alone,
Because I cannot love but one.

### 5

And I will cross the whitening foam,
And I will seek a foreign home;
Till I forget a false fair face,
I ne'er shall find a resting-place;
My own dark thoughts I cannot shun,
But ever love, and love but one.

### 6

The poorest, veriest wretch on earth
Still finds some hospitable hearth,
Where Friendship's or Love's softer glow
May smile in joy or soothe in woe;
But friend or leman I have none,
Because I cannot love but one.

### 7

I go—but wheresoe'er I flee
There's not an eye will weep for me;
There's not a kind congenial heart,
Where I can claim the meanest part;
Nor thou, who hast my hopes undone,
Wilt sigh, although I love but one.

## 8

To think of every early scene,
Of what we are, and what we've been,
Would whelm some softer hearts with woe—
But mine, alas! has stood the blow;
Yet still beats on as it begun,
And never truly loves but one.

## 9

And who that dear lov'd one may be,
Is not for vulgar eyes to see;
And why that early love was cross'd,
Thou know'st the best, I feel the most;
But few that dwell beneath the sun
Have lov'd so long, and lov'd but one.

## 10

I've tried another's fetters too,
With charms perchance as fair to view;
And I would fain have lov'd as well,
But some unconquerable spell
Forbade my bleeding breast to own
A kindred care for aught but one.

## 11

'Twould soothe to take one lingering view,
And bless thee in my last adieu;
Yet wish I not those eyes to weep
For him that wanders o'er the deep;
His home, his hope, his youth are gone,
Yet still he loves, and loves but one.

# Lines to Mr. Hodgson

### 1

Huzza! Hodgson, we are going,
    Our embargo's off at last;
Favourable breezes blowing
    Bend the canvas o'er the mast.
From aloft the signal's streaming,
    Hark! the farewell gun is fired;
Women screeching, tars blaspheming,
    Tell us that our time's expir'd.
        Here's a rascal
        Come to task all,
    Prying from the Custom-house;
      Trunks unpacking,
      Cases cracking—
    Not a corner for a mouse
'Scapes unsearched amid the racket,
Ere we sail on board the Packet.

### 2

Now our boatmen quit their mooring,
    And all hands must ply the oar;
Baggage from the quay is lowering,
    We're impatient, push from shore.
"Have a care! that case holds liquor—
    Stop the boat—I'm sick—oh Lord!"
"Sick, Ma'am, damme, you'll be sicker,

Ere you've been an hour on board."
    Thus are screaming
    Men and women,
Gemmen, ladies, servants, Jacks;
    Here entangling,
    All are wrangling,
Stuck together close as wax.—
Such the general noise and racket,
Ere we reach the Lisbon Packet.

3
Now we've reached her, lo! the Captain,
    Gallant Kidd, commands the crew;
Passengers their berths are clapt in,
    Some to grumble, some to spew.
"Hey day! call you that a cabin?
    Why 'tis hardly three feet square:
Not enough to stow Queen Mab in—
    Who the deuce can harbour there?"
      "Who, sir? plenty—
      Nobles twenty
Did at once my vessel fill."—
      "Did they? Jesus,
      How you squeeze us!
    Would to God they did so still:
Then I'd 'scape the heat and racket
Of the good ship, Lisbon Packet."

Fletcher! Murray! Bob! where are you?
    Stretched along the deck like logs—
Bear a hand, you jolly tar, you!
    Here's a rope's end for the dogs.
Hobhouse muttering fearful curses,
    As the hatchway down he rolls,
Now his breakfast, now his verses,
    Vomits forth—and damns our souls.
      "Here's a stanza
      On Braganza—
Help!"—"A couplet?"—"No, a cup
    Of warm water—"
    "What's the matter?"
"Zounds! my liver's coming up;
I shall not survive the racket
Of this brutal Lisbon Packet."


        5
Now at length we're off for Turkey,
    Lord knows when we shall come back!
Breezes foul and tempests murky
    May unship us in a crack.
But, since Life at most a jest is,
    As philosophers allow,
Still to laugh by far the best is,
    Then laugh on—as I do now.
      Laugh at all things,
      Great and small things,
Sick or well, at sea or shore;

While we're quaffing,
Let's have laughing—
Who the devil cares for more?—
Some good wine! and who would lack it,
Ev'n on board the Lisbon Packet?

# Stanzas Composed During A Thunderstorm

### 1

Chill and mirk is the nightly blast,
　Where Pindus' mountains rise,
And angry clouds are pouring fast
　The vengeance of the skies.

### 2

Our guides are gone, our hope is lost,
　And lightnings, as they play,
But show where rocks our path have crost,
　Or gild the torrent's spray.

### 3

Is yon a cot I saw, though low?
　When lightning broke the gloom—
How welcome were its shade!—ah, no!
　'Tis but a Turkish tomb.

### 4

Through sounds of foaming waterfalls,
　I hear a voice exclaim—
My way-worn countryman, who calls
　On distant England's name.

### 5

A shot is fired—by foe or friend?
　Another—'tis to tell
The mountain-peasants to descend,
　And lead us where they dwell.

### 6

Oh! who in such a night will dare
    To tempt the wilderness?
And who mid thunder-peals can hear
    Our signal of distress?

### 7

And who that heard our shouts would rise
    To try the dubious road?
Nor rather deem from nightly cries
    That outlaws were abroad.

### 8

Clouds burst, skies flash, oh, dreadful hour!
    More fiercely pours the storm!
Yet here one thought has still the power
    To keep my bosom warm.

### 9

While wandering through each broken path
    O'er brake and craggy brow;
While elements exhaust their wrath,
    Sweet Florence, where art thou?

### 10

Not on the sea, not on the sea—
    Thy bark hath long been gone:
Oh, may the storm that pours on me,
    Bow down my head alone!

### 11

Full swiftly blew the swift Siroc,
　　When last I pressed thy lip;
And long ere now, with foaming shock,
　　Impelled thy gallant ship.

### 12

Now thou art safe; nay, long ere now
　　Hast trod the shore of Spain;
'Twere hard if aught so fair as thou
　　Should linger on the main.

### 13

And since I now remember thee
　　In darkness and in dread,
As in those hours of revelry
　　Which Mirth and Music sped;

### 14

Do thou, amid the fair white walls,
　　If Cadiz yet be free,
At times from out her latticed halls
　　Look o'er the dark blue sea;

### 15

Then think upon Calypso's isles,
　　Endeared by days gone by;
To others give a thousand smiles,
　　To me a single sigh.

### 16

And when the admiring circle mark
  The paleness of thy face,
A half-formed tear, a transient spark
  Of melancholy grace,

### 17

Again thou'lt smile, and blushing shun
  Some coxcomb's raillery;
Nor own for once thou thought'st on one,
  Who ever thinks on thee.

### 18

Though smile and sigh alike are vain,
  When severed hearts repine
My spirit flies o'er Mount and Main
  And mourns in search of *thine*.

# Girl of Cadiz

### 1

Oh never talk again to me
    Of northern climes and British ladies;
It has not been your lot to see,
    Like me, the lovely Girl of Cadiz
Although her eye be not of blue,
    Nor fair her locks, like English lasses,
How far its own expressive hue
    The languid azure eye surpasses!

### 2

Prometheus-like, from heaven she stole
    The fire that through those silken lashes
In darkest glances seems to roll,
    From eyes that cannot hide their flashes:
And as along her bosom steal
    In lengthened flow her raven tresses,
You'd swear each clustering lock could feel,
    And curled to give her neck caresses.

### 3

Our English maids are long to woo,
    And frigid even in possession;
And if their charms be fair to view,
    Their lips are slow at Love's confession;
But, born beneath a brighter sun,
    For love ordained the Spanish maid is,
And who,—when fondly, fairly won,—
    Enchants you like the Girl of Cadiz?

### 4

The Spanish maid is no coquette,
  Nor joys to see a lover tremble,
And if she love, or if she hate,
  Alike she knows not to dissemble.
Her heart can ne'er be bought or sold—
  Howe'er it beats, it beats sincerely;
And, though it will not bend to gold,
  'Twill love you long and love you dearly.

### 5

The Spanish girl that meets your love
  Ne'er taunts you with a mock denial,
For every thought is bent to prove
  Her passion in the hour of trial.
When thronging foemen menace Spain,
  She dares the deed and shares the danger;
And should her lover press the plain,
  She hurls the spear, her love's avenger.

### 6

And when, beneath the evening star,
  She mingles in the gay Bolero,
Or sings to her attuned guitar
  Of Christian knight or Moorish hero,
Or counts her beads with fairy hand
  Beneath the twinkling rays of Hesper,
Or joins Devotion's choral band,
  To chaunt the sweet and hallowed vesper;—

In each, her charms the heart must move
  Of all who venture to behold her;
Then let not maids less fair reprove
  Because her bosom is not colder:
Through many a clime 'tis mine to roam
  Where many a soft and melting maid is,
But none abroad, and few at home,
  May match the dark-eyed Girl of Cadiz.

# Written After Swimming from Sestos to Abydos

## 1

If, in the month of dark December,
  Leander, who was nightly wont
(What maid will not the tale remember?)
  To cross thy stream, broad Hellespont!

## 2

If, when the wintry tempest roared,
  He sped to Hero, nothing loth,
And thus of old thy current poured,
  Fair Venus! how I pity both!

## 3

For *me*, degenerate modern wretch,
  Though in the genial month of May,
My dripping limbs I faintly stretch,
  And think I've done a feat to-day.

## 4

But since he crossed the rapid tide,
  According to the doubtful story,
To woo,—and—Lord knows what beside,
  And swam for Love, as I for Glory;

'Twere hard to say who fared the best:
   Sad mortals! thus the Gods still plague you!
He lost his labour, I my jest:
   For he was drowned, and I've the ague.

# Maid of Athens, ere we part

Ζωη μου, σαζ αγαπω.

### 1

Maid of Athens, ere we part,
Give, oh give back my heart!
Or, since that has left my breast,
Keep it now, and take the rest!
Hear my vow before I go,
Ζωη μου, σαζ αγαπω.

### 2

By those tresses unconfined,
Wooed by each Ægean wind;
By those lids whose jetty fringe
Kiss thy soft cheeks' blooming tinge;
By those wild eyes like the roe,
Ζωη μου, σαζ αγαπω.

### 3

By that lip I long to taste;
By that zone-encircled waist;
By all the token-flowers that tell
What words can never speak so well;
By Love's alternate joy and woe,
Ζωη μου, σαζ αγαπω.

### 4

Maid of Athens! I am gone:
Think of me, sweet! when alone.
Though I fly to Istambol,
Athens holds my heart and soul:
Can I cease to love thee? No!
Ζωη μου, σας αγαπω.

# Euthanasia

### 1

When Time, or soon or late, shall bring
  The dreamless sleep that lulls the dead,
Oblivion! may thy languid wing
  Wave gently o'er my dying bed!

### 2

No band of friends or heirs be there,
  To weep, or wish, the coming blow:
No maiden, with dishevelled hair,
  To feel, or feign, decorous woe.

### 3

But silent let me sink to Earth,
  With no officious mourners near
I would not mar one hour of mirth,
  Nor startle Friendship with a tear.

### 4

Yet Love, if Love in such an hour
  Could nobly check its useless sighs,
Might then exert its latest power
  In her who lives, and him who dies.

### 5

'Twere sweet, my Psyche! to the last
  Thy features still serene to see:
Forgetful of its struggles past,
  E'en Pain itself should smile on thee.

### 6

But vain the wish—for Beauty still
  Will shrink, as shrinks the ebbing breath;
And Woman's tears, produced at will,
  Deceive in life, unman in death.

### 7

Then lonely be my latest hour,
  Without regret, without a groan;
For thousands Death hath ceased to lower,
  And pain been transient or unknown.

### 8

"Aye, but to die, and go," alas!
  Where all have gone, and all must go!
To be the nothing that I was
  Ere born to life and living woe!

### 9

Count o'er the joys thine hours have seen,
  Count o'er thy days from anguish free,
And know, whatever thou hast been,
  'Tis something better not to be.

# The Spell Is Broke, the Charm Is Flown!

The spell is broke, the charm is flown!
  Thus is it with Life's fitful fever:
We madly smile when we should groan;
  Delirium is our best deceiver.
Each lucid interval of thought
  Recalls the woes of Nature's charter;
And *He* that acts as *wise men ought,*
  But *lives*—as saints have died—a martyr.

# By the Rivers of Babylon We Sat Down and Wept

### I

We sate down and wept by the waters
  Of Babel, and thought of the day
When our foe, in the hue of his slaughters,
  Made Salem's high places his prey;
And Ye, oh her desolate daughters!
  Were scattered all weeping away.

### II

While sadly we gazed on the river
  Which rolled on in freedom below,
They demanded the song; but, oh never
  That triumph the Stranger shall know!
May this right hand be withered for ever,
  Ere it string our high harp for the foe!

### III

On the willow that harp is suspended,
  Oh Salem! its sound should be free;
And the hour when thy glories were ended
  But left me that token of thee:
And ne'er shall its soft tones be blended
  With the voice of the Spoiler by me!

# Fare thee Well

*"Alas! they had been friends in youth;*
*But whispering tongues can poison truth:*
*And Constancy lives in realms above;*
*And Life is thorny; and youth is vain:*
*And to be wroth with one we love,*
*Doth work like madness in the brain;*

--------

*But never either found another*
*To free the hollow heart from paining—*
*They stood aloof, the scars remaining,*
*Like cliffs which had been rent asunder;*
*A dreary sea now flows between,*
*But neither heat, nor frost, nor thunder,*
*Shall wholly do away, I ween,*
*The marks of that which once hath been."*

—Coleridge's *Christabel*.

Fare thee well! and if for ever,
   Still for ever, fare *thee* well:
Even though unforgiving, never
   'Gainst thee shall my heart rebel.
Would that breast were bared before thee
   Where thy head so oft hath lain,
While that placid sleep came o'er thee
   Which thou ne'er canst know again:
Would that breast, by thee glanced over,
   Every inmost thought could show!

Then thou would'st at last discover
   'Twas not well to spurn it so.
Though the world for this commend thee—
   Though it smile upon the blow,
Even its praise must offend thee,
   Founded on another's woe:
Though my many faults defaced me,
   Could no other arm be found,
Than the one which once embraced me,
   To inflict a cureless wound?
Yet, oh yet, thyself deceive not—
   Love may sink by slow decay,
But by sudden wrench, believe not
   Hearts can thus be torn away:
Still thine own its life retaineth—
   Still must mine, though bleeding, beat;
And the undying thought which paineth
   Is—that we no more may meet.
These are words of deeper sorrow
   Than the wail above the dead;
Both shall live—but every morrow
   Wake us from a widowed bed.
And when thou would'st solace gather—
   When our child's first accents flow—
Wilt thou teach her to say "Father!"
   Though his care she must forego?
When her little hands shall press thee—
   When her lip to thine is pressed—
Think of him whose prayer shall bless thee—
   Think of him thy love *had* blessed!

Should her lineaments resemble
  Those thou never more may'st see,
Then thy heart will softly tremble
  With a pulse yet true to me.
All my faults perchance thou knowest—
  All my madness—none can know;
All my hopes—where'er thou goest—
  Wither—yet with *thee* they go.
Every feeling hath been shaken;
  Pride—which not a world could bow—
Bows to thee—by thee forsaken,
  Even my soul forsakes me now:
But 'tis done—all words are idle—
  Words from me are vainer still;
But the thoughts we cannot bridle
  Force their way without the will.
Fare thee well! thus disunited—
  Torn from every nearer tie—
Seared in heart—and lone—and blighted—
  More than this I scarce can die.

# Sonnet

Thy cheek is pale with thought, but not from woe,
  And yet so lovely, that if Mirth could flush
  Its rose of whiteness with the brightest blush,
My heart would wish away that ruder glow:
And dazzle not thy deep-blue eyes—but, oh!
  While gazing on them sterner eyes will gush,
  And into mine my mother's weakness rush,
Soft as the last drops round Heaven's airy bow.
For, through thy long dark lashes low depending,
  The soul of melancholy Gentleness
Gleams like a Seraph from the sky descending,
  Above all pain, yet pitying all distress;
At once such majesty with sweetness blending,
  I worship more, but cannot love thee less.

## On Being Asked What Was the "Origin of Love"

The "Origin of Love!"—Ah, why
   That cruel question ask of me,
When thou mayest read in many an eye
   He starts to life on seeing thee?
And shouldst thou seek his *end* to know:
   My heart forebodes, my fears foresee,
He'll linger long in silent woe;
   But live until—I cease to be.

# She Walks in Beauty

### I

She walks in Beauty, like the night
  Of cloudless climes and starry skies;
And all that's best of dark and bright
  Meet in her aspect and her eyes:
Thus mellowed to that tender light
  Which Heaven to gaudy day denies.

### II

One shade the more, one ray the less,
  Had half impaired the nameless grace
Which waves in every raven tress,
  Or softly lightens o'er her face;
Where thoughts serenely sweet express,
  How pure, how dear their dwelling-place.

### III

And on that cheek, and o'er that brow,
  So soft, so calm, yet eloquent,
The smiles that win, the tints that glow,
  But tell of days in goodness spent,
A mind at peace with all below,
  A heart whose love is innocent!

# The Destruction of Sennacherib

### I

The Assyrian came down like the wolf on the fold,
And his cohorts were gleaming in purple and gold;
And the sheen of their spears was like stars on the
      sea,
When the blue wave rolls nightly on deep Galilee.

### II

Like the leaves of the forest when Summer is green,
That host with their banners at sunset were seen:
Like the leaves of the forest when Autumn hath
      blown,
That host on the morrow lay withered and strown.

### III

For the angel of Death spread his wings on the
      blast,
And breathed in the face of the foe as he passed;
And the eyes of the sleepers waxed deadly and
      chill,
And their hearts but once heaved—and for ever
      grew still!

### IV

And there lay the steed with his nostrils all wide,
But through it there rolled not the breath of his
      pride;
And the foam of his gasping lay white on the turf,
And cold as the spray of the rock-beating surf.

### V

And there lay the rider distorted and pale,
With the dew on his brow, and the rust on his
          mail:
And the tents were all silent—the banners alone—
The lances unlifted—the trumpet unblown.

### VI

And the widows of Ashur are loud in their wail,
And the idols are broke in the temple of Baal;
And the might of the Gentile, unsmote by the
          sword,
Hath melted like snow in the glance of the Lord!

# Stanzas For Music

> "O Lachrymarum fons, tenero sacros
> Ducentium ortus ex animo: quater
>   Felix! in imo qui scatentem
>     Pectore te, pia Nympha Sensit."
>           —GRAY's *Poemata*.

### 1

There's not a joy the world can give like that it
        takes away,
When the glow of early thought declines in
        Feeling's dull decay;
'Tis not on Youth's smooth cheek the blush alone,
        which fades so fast,
But the tender bloom of heart is gone, ere Youth
        itself be past.

### 2

Then the few whose spirits float above the wreck
        of happiness
Are driven o'er the shoals of guilt or ocean of
        excess:
The magnet of their course is gone, or only points
        in vain
The shore to which their shivered sail shall never
        stretch again.

### 3

Then the mortal coldness of the soul like Death
        itself comes down;
It cannot feel for others' woes, it dare not dream its
        own;
That heavy chill has frozen o'er the fountain of our
        tears,
And though the eye may sparkle still, 'tis where
        the ice appears.

### 4

Though wit may flash from fluent lips, and mirth
        distract the breast,
Through midnight hours that yield no more their
        former hope of rest;
'Tis but as ivy-leaves around the ruined turret
        wreath,
All green and wildly fresh without, but worn and
        grey beneath.

### 5

Oh, could I feel as I have felt,—or be what I have
        been,
Or weep as I could once have wept, o'er many a
        vanished scene;
As springs, in deserts found, seem sweet, all
        brackish though they be,
So, midst the withered waste of life, those tears
        would flow to me.

# Song of Saul Before His Last Battle

### I

Warriors and Chiefs! should the shaft or the sword
Pierce me in leading the host of the Lord,
Heed not the corse, though a King's, in your path:
Bury your steel in the bosoms of Gath!

### II

Thou who art bearing my buckler and bow,
Should the soldiers of Saul look away from the foe,
Stretch me that moment in blood at thy feet!
Mine be the doom which they dared not to meet.

### III

Farewell to others, but never we part,
Heir to my Royalty—Son of my heart!
Bright is the diadem, boundless the sway,
Or kingly the death, which awaits us to-day!

# Saul

### I

Thou whose spell can raise the dead,
    Bid the Prophet's form appear:—
"Samuel, raise thy buried head!
    King, behold the phantom Seer!"
Earth yawned; he stood the centre of a cloud:
Light changed its hue, retiring from his shroud.
Death stood all glassy in his fixéd eye;
His hand was withered, and his veins were dry;
His foot, in bony whiteness, glittered there,
Shrunken and sinewless, and ghastly bare;
From lips that moved not and unbreathing frame,
Like caverned winds, the hollow acccents came.
Saul saw, and fell to earth, as falls the oak
At once, and blasted by the thunder-stroke.

### II

    "Why is my sleep disquieted?
    Who is he that calls the dead?
    Is it thou, O King? Behold,
Bloodless are these limbs, and cold:
Such are mine; and such shall be
Thine to-morrow, when with me:
Ere the coming day is done,
Such shalt thou be—such thy Son.
Fare thee well, but for a day,
Then we mix our mouldering clay.
Thou—thy race, lie pale and low,

Pierced by shafts of many a bow;
And the falchion by thy side
To thy heart thy hand shall guide:
Crownless—breathless—headless fall,
Son and sire—the house of Saul!"

# "All Is Vanity, Saith the Preacher"

## I

Fame, Wisdom, Love, and Power were mine,
    And Health and Youth possessed me;
My goblets blushed from every vine,
    And lovely forms caressed me;
I sunned my heart in Beauty's eyes,
    And felt my soul grow tender;
All Earth can give, or mortal prize,
    Was mine of regal splendour.

## II

I strive to number o'er what days
    Remembrance can discover,
Which all that Life or Earth displays
    Would lure me to live over.
There rose no day, there rolled no hour
    Of pleasure unembittered;
And not a trapping decked my Power
    That galled not while it glittered.

## III

The serpent of the field, by art
    And spells, is won from harming;
But that which coils around the heart,
    Oh! who hath power of charming?
It will not list to Wisdom's lore,
    Nor Music's voice can lure it;
But there it stings for evermore
    The soul that must endure it.

# When Coldness Wraps This Suffering Clay

### I

When coldness wraps this suffering clay,
    Ah! whither strays the immortal mind?
It cannot die, it cannot stay,
    But leaves its darkened dust behind.
Then, unembodied, doth it trace
    By steps each planet's heavenly way?
Or fill at once the realms of space,
    A thing of eyes, that all survey?

### II

Eternal—boundless,—undecayed,
    A thought unseen, but seeing all,
All, all in earth, or skies displayed,
    Shall it survey, shall it recall:
Each fainter trace that Memory holds
    So darkly of departed years,
In one broad glance the Soul beholds,
    And all, that was, at once appears.

### III

Before Creation peopled earth,
    Its eye shall roll through chaos back;
And where the farthest heaven had birth,
    The Spirit trace its rising track.
And where the future mars or makes,
    Its glance dilate o'er all to be,
While sun is quenched—or System breaks,
    Fixed in its own Eternity.

## IV

Above or Love—Hope—Hate—or Fear,
　　It lives all passionless and pure:
An age shall fleet like earthly year;
　　Its years as moments shall endure.
Away—away—without a wing,
　　O'er all—through all—its thought shall fly,
A nameless and eternal thing,
　　Forgetting what it was to die.

# On the Day of the Destruction of Jerusalem by Titus

## I

From the last hill that looks on thy once holy dome,
I behold thee, oh Sion! when rendered to Rome:
'Twas thy last sun went down, and the flames of
       thy fall
Flashed back on the last glance I gave to thy wall.

## II

I looked for thy temple—I look'd for my home,
And forgot for a moment my bondage to come;
I beheld but the death-fire that fed on thy fane,
And the fast-fettered hands that made vengence
       in vain.

## III

On many an eve, the high spot whence I gazed
Had reflected the last beam of day as it blazed;
While I stood on the height, and beheld the
       decline
Of the rays from the mountain that shone on thy
       shrine.

## IV

And now on that mountain I stood on that day,
But I marked not the twilight beam melting away;
Oh! would that the lightning had glared in its
       stead,

And the thunderbolt burst on the Conqueror's
      head!


V

But the Gods of the Pagan shall never profane
The shrine where Jehovah disdained not to reign;
And scattered and scorned as thy people may be,
Our worship, oh Father! is only for thee.

# Stanzas for Music

### 1

There be none of Beauty's daughters
  With a magic like thee;
And like music on the waters
  Is thy sweet voice to me:
When, as if its sound were causing
The charméd Ocean's pausing,
The waves lie still and gleaming,
And the lulled winds seem dreaming:

### 2

And the Midnight Moon is weaving
  Her bright chain o'er the deep;
Whose breast is gently heaving,
  As an infant's asleep:
So the spirit bows before thee,
To listen and adore thee;
With a full but soft emotion,
Like the swell of Summer's ocean.

# Darkness

I had a dream, which was not all a dream.
The bright sun was extinguished, and the stars
Did wander darkling in the eternal space,
Rayless, and pathless, and the icy Earth
Swung blind and blackening in the moonless air;
Morn came and went—and came, and brought no
         day,
And men forgot their passions in the dread
Of this their desolation; and all hearts
Were chilled into a selfish prayer for light:
And they did live by watchfires—and the thrones,
The palaces of crownéd kings—the huts,
The habitations of all things which dwell,
Were burnt for beacons; cities were consumed,
And men were gathered round their blazing homes
To look once more into each other's face;
Happy were those who dwelt within the eye
Of the volcanoes, and their mountain-torch:
A fearful hope was all the World contained;
Forests were set on fire—but hour by hour
They fell and faded—and the crackling trunks
Extinguished with a crash—and all was black.
The brows of men by the despairing light
Wore an unearthly aspect, as by fits
The flashes fell upon them; some lay down
And hid their eyes and wept; and some did rest
Their chins upon their clenchéd hands, and smiled;
And others hurried to and fro, and fed

Their funeral piles with fuel, and looked up
With mad disquietude on the dull sky,
The pall of a past World; and then again
With curses cast them down upon the dust,
And gnashed their teeth and howled: the wild
          birds shrieked,
And, terrified, did flutter on the ground
And flap their useless wings; the wildest brutes
Came tame and tremulous; and vipers crawled
And twined themselves among the multitude,
Hissing, but stingless—they were slain for food:
And War, which for a moment was no more,
Did glut himself again:—a meal was bought
With blood, and each sate sullenly apart
Gorging himself in gloom: no Love was left;
All earth was but one thought—and that was
          Death,
Immediate and inglorious; and the pang
Of famine fed upon all entrails—men
Died, and their bones were tombless as their flesh;
The meagre by the meagre were devoured,
Even dogs assailed their masters, all save one,
And he was faithful to a corse, and kept
The birds and beasts and famished men at bay,
Till hunger clung them, or the dropping dead
Lured their lank jaws; himself sought out no food,
But with a piteous and perpetual moan,
And a quick desolate cry, licking the hand
Which answered not with a caress—he died.
The crowd was famished by degrees; but two

Of an enormous city did survive,
And they were enemies: they met beside
The dying embers of an altar-place
Where had been heaped a mass of holy things
For an unholy usage; they raked up,
And shivering scraped with their cold skeleton
        hands
The feeble ashes, and their feeble breath
Blew for a little life, and made a flame
Which was a mockery; then they lifted up
Their eyes as it grew lighter, and beheld
Each other's aspects—saw, and shrieked, and died—
Even of their mutual hideousness they died,
Unknowing who he was upon whose brow
Famine had written Fiend. The World was void,
The populous and the powerful was a lump,
Seasonless, herbless, treeless, manless, lifeless—
A lump of death—a chaos of hard clay.
The rivers, lakes, and ocean all stood still,
And nothing stirred within their silent depths;
Ships sailorless lay rotting on the sea,
And their masts fell down piecemeal: as they
        dropped
They slept on the abyss without a surge—
The waves were dead; the tides were in their grave,
The Moon, their mistress, had expired before;
The winds were withered in the stagnant air,
And the clouds perished; Darkness had no need
Of aid from them—She was the Universe.

# Prometheus

## I

Titan! to whose immortal eyes
  The sufferings of mortality,
  Seen in their sad reality,
Were not as things that gods despise;
What was thy pity's recompense?
A silent suffering, and intense;
The rock, the vulture, and the chain,
All that the proud can feel of pain,
The agony they do not show,
The suffocating sense of woe,
  Which speaks but in its loneliness,
And then is jealous lest the sky
Should have a listener, nor will sigh
  Until its voice is echoless.

## II

Titan! to thee the strife was given
  Between the suffering and the will,
  Which torture where they cannot kill;
And the inexorable Heaven,
And the deaf tyranny of Fate,
The ruling principle of Hate,
Which for its pleasure doth create
The things it may annihilate,
Refused thee even the boon to die:
The wretched gift Eternity
Was thine—and thou hast borne it well.

All that the Thunderer wrung from thee
Was but the Menace which flung back
On him the torments of thy rack;
The fate thou didst so well foresee,
But would not to appease him tell;
And in thy Silence was his Sentence,
And in his Soul a vain repentance,
And evil dread so ill dissembled,
That in his hand the lightnings trembled.

### III

Thy Godlike crime was to be kind,
  To render with thy precepts less
  The sum of human wretchedness,
And strengthen Man with his own mind;
But baffled as thou wert from high,
Still in thy patient energy,
In the endurance, and repulse
  Of thine impenetrable Spirit,
Which Earth and Heaven could not convulse,
  A mighty lesson we inherit:
Thou art a symbol and a sign
  To Mortals of their fate and force;
Like thee, Man is in part divine,
  A troubled stream from a pure source;
And Man in portions can foresee
His own funereal destiny;
His wretchedness, and his resistance,
And his sad unallied existence:
To which his Spirit may oppose

Itself—an equal to all woes—
   And a firm will, and a deep sense,
Which even in torture can descry
   Its own concentered recompense,
Triumphant where it dares defy,
And making Death a Victory.

# Sonnet to Lake Leman

Rousseau—Voltaire—our Gibbon—De Staël—
  Leman! these names are worthy of thy shore,
  Thy shore of names like these! wert thou no
       more,
Their memory thy remembrance would recall:
To them thy banks were lovely as to all,
  But they have made them lovelier, for the lore
  Of mighty minds doth hallow in the core
Of human hearts the ruin of a wall
  Where dwelt the wise and wondrous; but by
       *thee*
How much more, Lake of Beauty! do we feel,
  In sweetly gliding o'er thy crystal sea,
The wild glow of that not ungentle zeal,
  Which of the Heirs of Immortality
Is proud, and makes the breath of Glory real!

# The Dream

## I

Our life is twofold: Sleep hath its own world,
A boundary between the things misnamed
Death and existence: Sleep hath its own world,
And a wide realm of wild reality,
And dreams in their development have breath,
And tears, and tortures, and the touch of Joy;
They leave a weight upon our waking thoughts,
They take a weight from off waking toils,
They do divide our being; they become
A portion of ourselves as of our time,
And look like heralds of Eternity;
They pass like spirits of the past,—they speak
Like Sibyls of the future; they have power—
The tyranny of pleasure and of pain;
They make us what we were not—what they will,
And shake us with the vision that's gone by,
The dread of vanished shadows—Are they so?
Is not the past all shadow?—What are they?
Creations of the mind?—The mind can make
Substances, and people planets of its own
With beings brighter than have been, and give
A breath to forms which can outlive all flesh.
I would recall a vision which I dreamed
Perchance in sleep—for, in itself, a thought,
A slumbering thought, is capable of years,
And curdles a long life into one hour.

## II

I saw two beings in the hues of youth
Standing upon a hill, a gentle hill,
Green and of mild declivity, the last
As 'twere the cape of a long ridge of such,
Save that there was no sea to lave its base,
But a most living landscape, and the wave
Of woods and corn-fields, and the abodes of men
Scattered at intervals, and wreathing smoke
Arising from such rustic roofs;—the hill
Was crowned with a peculiar diadem
Of trees, in circular array, so fixed,
Not by the sport of nature, but of man:
These two, a maiden and a youth, were there
Gazing—he one on all that was beneath
Fair as herself—but the Boy gazed on her;
And both were young, and one was beautiful:
And both were young—yet not alike in youth.
As the sweet moon on the horizon's verge,
The Maid was on the eve of Womanhood;
The Boy had fewer summers, but his heart
Had far outgrown his years, and to his eye
There was but one belovéd face on earth,
And that was shining on him: he had looked
Upon it till it could not pass away;
He had no breath, no being, but in hers;
She was his voice; he did not speak to her,
But trembled on her words; she was his sight,
For his eye followed hers, and saw with hers,
Which coloured all his objects:—he had ceased

To live within himself; she was his life,
The ocean to the river of his thoughts,
Which terminated all: upon a tone,
A touch of hers, his blood would ebb and flow,
And his cheek change tempestuously—his heart
Unknowing of its cause of agony.
But she in these fond feelings had no share:
Her sighs were not for him; to her he was
Even as a brother—but no more; 'twas much,
For brotherless she was, save in the name
Her infant friendship had bestowed on him;
Herself the solitary scion left
Of a time-honoured race.—It was a name
Which pleased him, and yet pleased him not—and
            why?
Time taught him a deep answer—when she loved
Another; even *now* she loved another,
And on the summit of that hill she stood
Looking afar if yet her lover's steed
Kept pace with her expectancy, and flew.


III
A change came o'er the spirit of my dream.
There was an ancient mansion, and before
Its walls there was a steed caparisoned:
Within an antique Oratory stood
The Boy of whom I spake;—he was alone,
And pale, and pacing to and fro: anon
He sate him down, and seized a pen, and traced
Words which I could not guess of; then he leaned

His bowed head on his hands, and shook as 'twere
With a convulsion—then rose again,
And with his teeth and quivering hands did tear
What he had written, but he shed no tears.
And he did calm himself, and fix his brow
Into a kind of quiet: as he paused,
The Lady of his love re-entered there;
She was serene and smiling then, and yet
She knew she was by him beloved—she knew,
For quickly comes such knowledge, that his heart
Was darkened with her shadow, and she saw
That he was wretched, but she saw not all.
He rose, and with a cold and gentle grasp
He took her hand; a moment o'er his face
A tablet of unutterable thoughts
Was traced, and then it faded, as it came;
He dropped the hand he held, and with slow
       steps
Retired, but not as bidding her adieu,
For they did part with mutual smiles; he passed
From out the massy gate of that old Hall,
And mounting on his steed he went his way;
And ne'er repassed that hoary threshold more.


IV
A change came o'er the spirit of my dream.
The Boy was sprung to manhood: in the wilds
Of fiery climes he made himself a home,
And his Soul drank their sunbeams: he was girt
With strange and dusky aspects; he was not

Himself like what he had been; on the sea
And on the shore he was a wanderer;
There was a mass of many images
Crowded like waves upon me, but he was
A part of all; and in the last he lay
Reposing from the noontide sultriness,
Couched among fallen columns, in the shade
Of ruined walls that had survived the names
Of those who reared them; by his sleeping side
Stood camels grazing, and some goodly steeds
Were fastened near a fountain; and a man
Clad in a flowing garb did watch the while,
While many of his tribe slumbered around:
And they were canopied by the blue sky,
So cloudless, clear, and purely beautiful,
That God alone was to be seen in Heaven.

V

A change came o'er the spirit of my dream.
The Lady of his love was wed with One
Who did not love her better:—in her home,
A thousand leagues from his,—her native home,
She dwelt, begirt with growing Infancy,
Daughters and sons of Beauty,—but behold!
Upon her face there was the tint of grief,
The settled shadow of an inward strife,
And an unquiet drooping of the eye,
As if its lid were charged with unshed tears.
What could her grief be?—she had all she loved,
And he who had so loved her was not there

To trouble with bad hopes, or evil wish,
Or ill-repressed affliction, her pure thoughts.
What could her grief be?—she had loved him not,
Nor given him cause to deem himself beloved,
Nor could he be a part of that which preyed
Upon her mind—a spectre of the past.

## VI

A change came o'er the spirit of my dream.
The Wanderer was returned.—I saw him stand
Before an Altar—with a gentle bride;
Her face was fair, but was not that which made
The Starlight of his Boyhood;—as he stood
Even at the altar, o'er his brow there came
The self-same aspect, and the quivering shock
That in the antique Oratory shook
His bosom in its solitude; and then—
As in that hour—a moment o'er his face
The tablet of unutterable thoughts
Was traced,—and then it faded as it came,
And he stood calm and quiet, and he spoke
The fitting vows, but heard not his own words,
And all things reeled around him; he could see
Not that which was, nor that which should have
          been—
But the old mansion, and the accustomed hall,
And the remembered chambers, and the place,
The day, the hour, the sunshine, and the shade,
All things pertaining to that place and hour,
And her who was his destiny, came back

And thrust themselves between him and the
       light;
What business had they there at such a time?

## VII

A change came o'er the spirit of my dream.
The Lady of his love;—Oh! she was changed,
As by the sickness of the soul; her mind
Had wandered from its dwelling, and her eyes,
They had not their own lustre, but the look
Which is not of the earth; she was become
The Queen of a fantastic realm; her thoughts
Were combinations of disjointed things;
And forms, impalpable and unperceived
Of others' sight, familiar were to hers.
And this the world calls frenzy; but the wise
Have a far deeper madness—and the glance
Of melancholy is a fearful gift;
What is it but the telescope of truth?
Which strips the distance of its fantasies,
And brings life near in utter nakedness,
Making the cold reality too real!

## VIII

A change came o'er the spirit of my dream.
The Wanderer was alone as heretofore,
The beings which surrounded him were gone,
Or were at war with him; he was a mark
For blight and desolation, compassed round
With Hatred and Contention; Pain was mixed

In all which was served up to him, until,
Like to the Pontic monarch of old days,
He fed on poisons, and they had no power,
But were a kind of nutriment; he lived
Through that which had been death to many men,
And made him friends of mountains: with the stars
And the quick Spirit of the Universe
He held his dialogues; and they did teach
To him the magic of their mysteries;
To him the book of Night was opened wide,
And voices from the deep abyss revealed
A marvel and a secret—Be it so.


IX

My dream is past; it had no further change.
It was of a strange order, that the doom
Of these two creatures should be thus traced out
Almost like a reality—the one
To end in madness—both in misery.

# The Prisoner of Chillon

Eternal Spirit of the chainless Mind!
  Brightest in dungeons, Liberty! thou art:
  For there thy habitation is the heart—
The heart which love of thee alone can bind;
And when thy sons to fetters are consigned—
  To fetters, and the damp vault's dayless gloom,
  Their country conquers with their martyrdom,
And Freedom's fame finds wings on every wind.
Chillon! thy prison is a holy place,
  And thy sad floor an altar—for 'twas trod,
Until his very step have left a trace
  Worn, as if thy cold pavement were a sod,
By Bonnivard!—May none those marks efface!
  For they appeal from tyranny to God.

### I

My hair is grey, but not with years,
Nor grew it white
    In a single night,
As men's have grown from sudden fears:
My limbs are bowed, though not with toil,
  But rusted with a vile repose,
For they have been a dungeon's spoil,
  And mine has been the fate of those
To whom the goodly earth and air
Are banned, and barred—forbidden fare;

But this was for my father's faith
I suffered chains and courted death;
That father perished at the stake
For tenets he would not forsake;
And for the same his lineal race
In darkness found a dwelling place;
We were seven—who now are one,
   Six in youth, and one in age,
Finished as they had begun,
   Proud of Persecution's rage;
One in fire, and two in field,
Their belief with blood have sealed,
Dying as their father died,
For the God their foes denied;—
Three were in a dungeon cast,
Of whom this wreck is left the last.


## II
There are seven pillars of Gothic mould,
In Chillon's dungeons deep and old,
There are seven columns, massy and grey,
Dim with a dull imprisoned ray,
A sunbeam which hath lost its way,
And through the crevice and the cleft
Of the thick wall is fallen and left;
Creeping o'er the floor so damp,
Like a marsh's meteor lamp:
And in each pillar there is a ring,
   And in each ring there is a chain;
That iron is a cankering thing,

For in these limbs its teeth remain,
With marks that will not wear away,
TIll I have done with this new day,
Which now is painful to these eyes,
Which have not seen the sun so rise
For years—I cannot count them o'er,
I lost their long and heavy score
When my last brother dropped and died,
And I lay living by his side.

## III

They chained us each to a column stone,
And we were three—yet, each alone;
We could not move a single pace,
We could not see each other's face,
But with that pale and livid light
That made us strangers in our sight:
And thus together—yet apart,
Fettered in hand, but joined in heart,
'Twas still some solace in the dearth
Of the pure elements of earth,
To hearken to each other's speech,
And each turn comforter to each
With some new hope, or legend old,
So song heroically bold;
But even these at length grew cold.
Our voices took a dreary tone,
An echo of the dungeon stone,
   A grating sound, not full and free,
   As they of yore were wont to be:

It might be fancy—but to me
They never sounded like our own.


IV

I was the eldest of the three,
   And to uphold and cheer the rest
   I ought to do—and did my best—
And each did well in his degree.
   The youngest, whom my father loved,
Because our mother's brow was given
To him, with eyes as blue as heaven—
   For him my soul was sorely moved:
And truly might it be distressed
To see such a bird in such a nest;
For he was as beautiful as day—
   (When day was beautiful to me
   As to young eagles, being free)—
   A polar day, which will not see
A sunset till its summer's gone,
   Its sleepless summer of long light,
The snow-clad offspring of the sun:
And thus he was as pure and bright,
And in his natural spirit gay,
With tears for nought but others' ills,
And then they flow'd like mountain rills,
Unless he could assuage the woe
Which he abhorred to view below.

The other was as pure of mind,
But formed to combat with his kind;
Strong in his frame, and of a mood
Which 'gainst the world in war had stood.
And perished in the foremost rank
   With joy:—but not in chains to pine:
His spirit withered with their clank,
   I saw it silently decline—
   And so perchance in sooth did mine:
But yet I forced it on to cheer
Those relics of a home so dear.
He was a hunter of the hills,
   Had followed there the deer and wolf
   To him this dungeon was a gulf,
And fettered feet the worst of ills.


VI
   Lake Leman lies by Chillon's walls:
A thousand feet in depth below
Its massy waters meet and flow;
Thus much the fathom-line was sent
From Chillon's snow-white battlement,
   Which round about the wave inthralls:
A double dungeon wall and wave
Have made—and like a living grave.
Below the surface of the lake
The dark vault lies wherein we lay:
We heard it ripple night and day;

Sounding o'er our heads it knocked;
And I have felt the winter's spray
Wash through the bars when winds were high
And wanton in the happy sky;
  And then the very rock hath rocked,
  And I have felt it shake, unshocked,
Because I could have smiled to see
The death that would have set me free.


## VII

I said my nearer brother pined,
I said his mighty heart declined,
He loathed and put away his food;
It was not that 'twas coarse and rude,
For we were used to hunter's fare,
And for the like had little care:
The milk drawn from the mountain goat
Was changed for water from the moat,
Our bread was such as captives' tears
Have moistened many a thousand years,
Since man first pent his fellow men
Like brutes within an iron den;
But what were these to us or him?
These wasted not his heart or limb;
My brother's soul was of that mould
Which in a palace had grown cold,
Had his free breathing been denied
The range of the steep mountain's side;
But why delay the truth?—he died.
I saw, and could not hold his head,

Nor reach his dying hand—nor dead,—
Though hard I strove, but strove in vain
To rend and gnash my bonds in twain.
He died—and they unlocked his chain,
And scooped for him a shallow grave
Even from the cold earth of our cave.
I begg'd them, as a boon, to lay
His corse in dust whereon the day
Might shine—it was a foolish thought,
But then within my brain it wrought,
That even in death his freeborn breast
In such a dungeon could not rest.
I might have spared my idle prayer—
They coldly laughed—and laid him there:
The flat and turfless earth above
The being we so much did love;
His empty chain above it leant,
Such Murder's fitting monument!

### VIII

But he, the favourite and the flower,
Most cherished since his natal hour,
His mother's image in fair face
The infant love of all his race
His martyred father's dearest thought,
My latest care, for whom I sought
To hoard my life, that his might be
Less wretched now, and one day free;
He, too, who yet had held untired
A spirit natural or inspired—

He, too, was struck, and day by day
Was withered on the stalk away.
Oh, God! it is a fearful thing
To see the human soul take wing
In any shape, in any mood:
I've seen it rushing forth in blood,
I've seen it on the breaking ocean
Strive with a swoln convulsive motion,
I've seen the sick and ghastly bed
Of Sin delirious with its dread:
But these were horrors—this was woe
Unmixed with such—but sure and slow:
He faded, and so calm and meek,
So softly worn, so sweetly weak,
So tearless, yet so tender—kind,
And grieved for those he left behind;
With all the while a cheek whose bloom
Was as a mockery of the tomb,
Whose tints as gently sunk away
As a departing rainbow's ray;
An eye of most transparent light,
That almost made the dungeon bright;
And not a word of murmur—not
A groan o'er his untimely lot,—
A little talk of better days,
A little hope my own to raise,
For I was sunk in silence—lost
In this last loss, of all the most;
And then the sighs he would suppress
Of fainting Nature's feebleness,

More slowly drawn, grew less and less:
I listened, but I could not hear;
I call'd, for I was wild with fear;
I knew 'twas hopeless, but my dread
Would not be thus admonishéd;
I called, and thought I heard a sound—
I burst my chain with one strong bound,
And rushed to him:—I found him not,
*I* only stirred in this black spot,
*I* only lived, *I* only drew
The accurséd breath of dungeon-dew;
The last, the sole, the dearest link
Between me and the eternal brink,
Which bound me to my failing race,
Was broken in this fatal place.
One on earth, and one beneath—
My brothers—both had ceased to breathe!
I took that hand which lay so still,
Alas! my own was full as chill;
I had not the strength to stir, or strive,
But felt that I was still alive—
A frantic feeling, when we know
That what we love shall ne'er be so.
    I know not why
      I could not die,
I had no earthly hope—but faith,
And that forbade a selfish death.

## IX

What next befell me then and there
  I know not well—I never knew—
First came the loss of light, and air,
  And then of darkness too:
I had no thought, no feeling—none—
Among the stones I stood a stone,
And was, scarce conscious what I wist,
As shrubless crags within the mist;
For all was blank, and bleak, and grey;
It was not night—it was not day;
It was not even the dungeon-light,
So hateful to my heavy sight,
But vacancy absorbing space,
And fixedness—without a place;
There were no stars—no earth—no time—
No check—no change—no good—no crime—
But silence, and a stirless breath
Which neither was of life nor death;
A sea of stagnant idleness,
Blind, boundless, mute, and motionless!

## X

A light broke in upon my brain,—
  It was the carol of a bird;
It ceased, and then it came again,
  The sweetest song ear ever heard,
And mine was thankful till my eyes
Ran over with the glad surprise,
And they that moment could not see

I was the mate of misery;
But then by dull degrees came back
My senses to their wonted track;
I saw the dungeon walls and floor
Close slowly round me as before,
I saw the glimmer of the sun
Creeping as it before had done,
But through the crevice where it came
That bird was perched, as fond and tame,
   And tamer than upon the tree;
A lovely bird, with azure wings,
And song that said a thousand things,
   And seemed to say them all for me!
I never saw its like before,
I ne'er shall see its likeness more:
It seemed like me to want a mate,
But was not half so desolate,
And it was come to love me when
None lived to love me so again,
And cheering from my dungeon's brink,
Had brought me back to feel and think.
I know not if it late were free,
   Or broke its cage to perch on mine,
But knowing well captivity,
   Sweet bird! I could not wish for thine!
Or if it were, in wingéd guise,
A visitant from Paradise;
For—Heaven forgive that thought! the while
Which made me both to weep and smile—
I sometimes deemed that it might be

My brother's soul come down to me;
But then at last away it flew,
And then 'twas mortal well I knew,
For he would never thus have flown—
And left me twice so doubly lone,—
Lone—as the corse within its shroud,
Lone—as a solitary cloud,
   A single cloud on a sunny day,
While all the rest of heaven is clear,
A frown upon the atmosphere,
That hath no business to appear
   When skies are blue, and earth is gay.


XI

A kind of change came in my fate,
My keepers grew compassionate;
I know not what had made them so,
They were inured to sights of woe,
But so it was:—my broken chain
With links unfastened did remain,
And it was to liberty to stride
Along my cell from side to side,
And up and down, and then athwart,
And tread it over every part;
And round the pillars one by one,
Returning where my walk begun,
Avoiding only, as I trod,
My brothers' graves without a sod;
For if I thought with heedless tread
My step profaned their lowly bed,

My breath came gaspingly and thick,
And my crushed heart felt blind and sick.

### XII

I made a footing in the wall,
　　It was not therefrom to escape,
For I had buried one and all
　　Who loved me in a human shape;
And the whole earth would henceforth be
A wider prison unto me:
No child—no sire—no kin had I,
No partner in my misery;
I thought of this, and I was glad,
For thought of them had made me mad;
But I was curious to ascend
To my barred windows, and to bend
Once more, upon the mountains high,
The quiet of a loving eye.

### XIII

I saw them—and they were the same,
They were not changed like me in frame;
I saw their thousand years of snow
On high—their wide long lake below,
And the blue Rhone in fullest flow;
I heard the torrents leap and gush
O'er channelled rock and broken bush;
I saw the white-walled distant town,
And whiter sails go skimming down;
And then there was a little isle,

Which in my very face did smile,
    The only one in view;
A small green isle, it seemed no more,
Scarce broader than my dungeon floor,
But in it there were three tall trees,
And o'er it blew the mountain breeze,
And by it there were waters flowing,
And on it there were young flowers growing,
    Of gentle breath and hue.
The fish swam by the castle wall,
And they seemed joyous each and all;
The eagle rode the rising blast,
Methought he never flew so fast
As then to me he seemed to fly;
And then new tears came in my eye,
And I felt troubled—and would fain
I had not left my recent chain;
And when I did descend again,
The darkness of my dim abode
Fell on me as a heavy load;
It was as is a new-dug grave,
Closing o'er one we sought to save,—
And yet my glance, too much opprest,
Had almost need of such a rest.

XIV

It might be months, or years, or days—
    I kept no count, I took no note—
I had no hope my eyes to raise,
    And clear them of their dreary mote;

At last men came to set me free;
   I asked not why, and recked not where;
It was at length the same to me,
Fettered or fetterless to be,
   I learned to love despair.
And thus when they appeared at last,
And all my bonds aside were cast,
These heavy walls to me had grown
A hermitage—and all my own!
And half I felt as they were come
To tear me from a second home:
With spiders I had friendship made,
And watch'd them in their sullen trade,
Had seen the mice by moonlight play,
And why should I feel less than they?
We were all inmates of one place,
And I, the monarch of each race,
Had power to kill—yet, strange to tell!
In quiet we had learn'd to dwell;
My very chains and I grew friends,
So much a long communion tends
To make us what we are;—even I
Regained my freedom with a sigh.

# Song for the Luddites

## 1

As the Liberty lads o'er the sea
Brought their freedom, and cheaply, with blood,
  So we, boys, we
 Will *die* fighting, or *live* free,
And down with all kings but King Ludd!

## 2

When the web that we weave is complete,
And the shuttle exchanged for the sword,
  We will fling the winding-sheet
 O'er the despot at our feet,
And dye it deep in the gore he has poured.

## 3

Though black as his heart its hue,
Since his veins are corrupted to mud,
  Yet this is the dew
 Which the tree shall renew
Of Liberty, planted by Ludd!

# Oh! Weep for Those

Oh! weep for those that wept by Babel's stream,
Whose shrines are desolate, whose land a dream;
Weep for the harp of Judah's broken shell;
Mourn—where their God hath dwelt the godless
      dwell!

II

And where shall Israel lave her bleeding feet?
And when shall Zion's songs again seem sweet?
And Judah's melody once more rejoice
The hearts that leaped before its heavenly voice?

III

Tribes of the wandering foot and weary breast,
How shall ye flee away and be at rest!
The wild-dove hath her nest, the fox his cave,
Mankind their country—Israel but the grave!

# Oh! Snatched Away in Beauty's Bloom

### I

Oh! snatched away in Beauty's bloom,
On thee shall press no ponderous tomb;
   But on thy turf shall roses rear
   Their leaves, the earliest of the year;
And the wild cypress wave in tender gloom:

### II

And oft by yon blue gushing stream
   Shall Sorrow lean her drooping head,
And feed deep thought with many a dream,
   And lingering pause and lightly tread;
Fond wretch! as if her step disturbed the dead!

### III

Away! we know that tears are vain,
   That Death nor heeds nor hears distress:
Will this unteach us to complain?
   Or make one mourner weep the less?
And thou—who tell'st me to forget—
Thy looks are wan, thine eyes are wet.

# My Soul is Dark

### I

My soul is dark—Oh! quickly string
   The harp I yet can brook to hear;
And let thy gentle fingers fling
   Its melting murmurs o'er mine ear.
If in this heart a hope be dear,
   That sound shall charm it forth again:
If in these eyes there lurk a tear
   'Twill flow, and cease to burn my brain.


### II

But bid the strain be wild and deep,
   Nor let thy notes of joy be first:
I tell thee, minstrel, I must weep,
   Or else this heavy heart will burst;
For it hath been by sorrow nursed,
   And ached in sleepless silence long;
And now 'tis doomed to know the worst,
   And break at once—or yield to song.

# I Saw Thee Weep

### I

I saw thee weep—the big bright tear
   Came o'er that eye of blue;
And then, methought, it did appear
   A violet dropping dew:
I saw thee smile—the sapphire's blaze
   Beside thee ceased to shine;
It could not match the living rays
   That filled that glance of thine.

### II

As clouds from yonder sun receive
   A deep and mellow dye,
Which scarce the shade of coming eve
   Can banish from the sky,
Those smiles unto the moodiest mind
   Their own pure joy impart;
Their sunshine leaves a glow behind
   That lightens o'er the heart.

# Thy Days Are Done

### I

Thy days are done, thy fame begun;
  Thy country's strains record
The triumphs of her chosen Son,
  The slaughters of his sword!
The deeds he did, the fields he won,
  The freedom he restored!

### II

Though thou art fall'n, while we are free
  Thou shalt not taste of death!
The generous blood that flowed from thee
  Disdained to sink beneath:
Within our veins its currents be,
  Thy spirit on our breath!

### III

Thy name, our charging hosts along,
  Shall be the battle-word!
Thy fall, the theme of choral song
  From virgin voices poured!
To weep would do thy glory wrong:
  Thou shalt not be deplored.

# Sun of the Sleepless!

Sun of the sleepless! melancholy star!
Whose tearful beam glows tremulously far,
That show'st the darkness thou canst not dispel,
How like art thou to Joy remembered well!
So gleams the past, the light of other days,
Which shines, but warms not with its powerless
        rays:
A night-beam, Sorrow watcheth to behold,
Distinct, but distant—clear—but, oh how cold!

# So We'll Go No More A-Roving

### 1
So we'll go no more a-roving
  So late into the night,
Though the heart be still as loving,
  And the moon be still as bright.

### 2
For the sword outwears its sheath,
  And the soul wears out the breast,
And the heart must pause to breathe,
  And Love itself have rest.

### 3
Though the night was made for loving,
  And the day returns too soon,
Yet we'll go no more a-roving
  By the light of the moon.

# Manfred

When the Moon is on the wave,
  And the glow-worm in the grass,
And the meteor on the grave,
  And the wisp on the morass;
When the falling stars are shooting,
And the answered owls are hooting,
And the silent leaves are still
In the shadow of the hill,
Shall my soul be upon thine,
With a power and with a sign.

Though thy slumber may be deep,
Yet thy Spirit shall not sleep;
There are shades which will not vanish,
There are thoughts thou canst not banish;
By a Power to thee unknown,
Thou canst never be alone;
Thou art wrapt as with a shroud,
Thou art gathered in a cloud;
And for ever shalt thou dwell
In the spirit of this spell.

Though thou seest me not pass by,
Thou shalt feel me with thine eye
As a thing that, though unseen,
Must be near thee, and hath been;

And when in that secret dread
Thou hast turned around thy head,
Thou shalt marvel I am not
As thy shadow on the spot,
And the power which thou dost feel
Shall be what thou must conceal.

And a magic voice and verse
Hath baptized thee with a curse;
And a Spirit of the air
Hath begirt thee with a snare;
In the wind there is a voice
Shall forbid thee to rejoice;
And to thee shall Night deny
All the quiet of her sky;
And the day shall have a sun,
Which shall make thee wish it done.

From thy false tears I did distil
An essence which hath strength to kill;
From thy own heart I then did wring
The black blood in its blackest spring;
From thy own smile I snatched the snake,
For there it coiled as in a brake;
From thy own lip I drew the charm
Which gave all these their chiefest harm;
In proving every poison known,
I found the strongest was thine own.

By thy cold breast and serpent smile,
By thy unfathomed gulfs of guile,
By that most seeming virtuous eye,
By thy shut soul's hypocrisy;
By the perfection of thine art
Which passed for human thine own heart;
By thy delight in others' pain,
And by thy brotherhood of Cain,
I call upon thee! and compel
Thyself to be thy proper Hell!

And on thy head I pour the vial
Which doth devote thee to this trial;
Nor to slumber, nor to die,
Shall be in thy destiny;
Though thy death shall still seem near
To thy wish, but as a fear;
Lo! the spell now works around thee,
And the clankless chain hath bound thee;
O'er thy heart and brain together
Hath the word been passed—now wither!

# Don Juan

*Difficile est propriè communia dicere.*
                                    HORACE.

*Dost thou think, because thou art virtuous, there shall
be no more cakes and ale? Yes, by Saint Anne, and
ginger shall be hot i' the mouth, too!*
        Shakespeare, Twelfth Night, or What You Will

## DEDICATION

### I

Bob Southey! You're a poet—Poet-laureate,
    And representative of all the race,
Although 'tis true that you turned out a Tory at
    Last,—yours has lately been a common case,—
And now, my Epic Renegade! what are ye at?
    With all the Lakers, in and out of place?
A nest of tuneful persons, to my eye
Like "four and twenty Blackbirds in a pye;

### II

"Which pye being opened they began to sing"
    (This old song and new simile holds good),
"A dainty dish to set before the King,"
    Or Regent, who admires such kind of food;—
And Coleridge, too, has lately taken wing,
    But like a hawk encumber'd with his hood,—
Explaining metaphysics to the nation—
I wish he would explain his Explanation.

### III

You, Bob! are rather insolent, you know,
  At being disappointed in your wish
To supersede all warblers here below,
  And be the only Blackbird in the dish;
And then you overstrain yourself, or so,
  And tumble downward like the flying fish
Gasping on deck, because you soar too high, Bob,
And fall, for lack of moisture quite a-dry, Bob!

### IV

And Wordsworth, in a rather long *Excursion*
  (I think the quarto holds five hundred pages),
Has given a sample from the vasty version
  Of his new system to perplex the sages;
'Tis poetry—at least by his assertion,
  And may appear so when the dog-star rages—
And he who understands it would be able
To add a story to the Tower of Babel.

### V

You—Gentlemen! by dint of long seclusion
  From better company, have kept your own
At Keswick, and, through still continued fusion
  Of one another's minds, at last have grown
To deem as a most logical conclusion,
  That Poesy has wreaths for you alone:
There is a narrowness in such a notion,
Which makes me wish you'd change your lakes for
        ocean.

## VI

I would not imitate the petty thought,
  Nor coin my self-love to so base a vice,
For all the glory your conversion brought,
  Since gold alone should not have been its price.
You have your salary; was't for that you wrought?
  And Wordsworth has his place in the Excise.
You're shabby fellows—true—but poets still,
And duly seated on the immortal hill.

## VII

Your bays may hide the baldness of your brows—
  Perhaps some virtuous blushes;—let them go—
To you I envy neither fruit nor boughs—
  And for the fame you would engross below,
The field is universal, and allows
  Scope to all such as feel the inherent glow:
Scott, Rogers, Campbell, Moore, and Crabbe, will
      try
'Gainst you the question with posterity.

## VIII

For me, who, wandering with pedestrian Muses,
  Contend not with you on the wingèd steed,
I wish your fate may yield ye, when she chooses,
  The fame you envy, and the skill you need;
And recollect a poet nothing loses
  In giving to his brethren their full meed
Of merit, and complaint of present days
Is not the certain path to future praise.

## IX

He that reserves his laurels for posterity
   (Who does not often claim the bright reversion)
Has generally no great crop to spare it, he
   Being only injured by his own assertion;
And although here and there some glorious rarity
   Arise like Titan from the sea's immersion,
The major part of such appellants go
To—God knows where—for no one else can know.

## X

If, fallen in evil days on evil tongues,
   Milton appeal'd to the Avenger, Time,
If Time, the Avenger, execrates his wrongs,
   And makes the word "Miltonic" mean "*sublime*,"
*He* deign'd not to belie his soul in songs,
   Nor turn his very talent to a crime;
*He* did not loathe the Sire to laud the Son,
But closed the tyrant-hater he begun.

## XI

Think'st thou, could he—the blind Old Man—arise,
   Like Samuel from the grave, to freeze once more
The blood of monarchs with his prophecies,
   Or be alive again—again all hoar
With time and trials, and those helpless eyes,
   And heartless daughters—worn—and pale—and
          poor;
Would *he* adore a sultan? *he* obey
The intellectual eunuch Castlereagh?

## XII

Cold-blooded, smooth-faced, placid miscreant!
　　Dabbling its sleek young hands in Erin's gore,
And thus for wider carnage taught to pant,
　　Transferred to gorge upon a sister shore,
The vulgarest tool that Tyranny could want,
　　With just enough of talent, and no more,
To lengthen fetters by another fixed,
And offer poison long already mixed.

## XIII

An orator of such set trash of phrase
　　Ineffably—legitimately vile,
That even its grossest flatterers dare not praise,
　　Nor foes—all nations—condescend to smile,—
Not even a sprightly blunder's spark can blaze
　　From that Ixion grindstone's ceaseless toil,
That turns and turns to give the world a notion
Of endless torments and perpetual motion.

## XIV

A bungler even in its disgusting trade,
　　And botching, patching, leaving still behind
Something of which its masters are afraid,
　　States to be curbed, and thoughts to be confined,
　　Conspiracy or Congress to be made—
Cobbling at manacles for all mankind—
A tinkering slave-maker, who mends old chains,
With God and Man's abhorrence for its gains.

## XV

If we may judge of matter by the mind,
  Emasculated to the marrow *It*
Hath but two objects, how to serve, and bind,
  Deeming the chain it wears even men may fit,
Eutropius of its many masters,—blind
  To worth as freedom, wisdom as to wit,
Fearless—because *no* feeling dwells in ice,
Its very courage stagnates to a vice.


## XVI

Where shall I turn me not to *view* its bonds,
  For I will never *feel* them;—Italy!
Thy late reviving Roman soul desponds
  Beneath the lie this State-thing breathed o'er
      thee—
Thy clanking chain, and Erin's yet green wounds,
  Have voices—tongues to cry aloud for me.
Europe has slaves, allies, kings, armies still,
And Southey lives to sing them very ill.


## XVII

Meantime, Sir Laureate, I proceed to dedicate,
  In honest simple verse, this song to you,
And, if in flattering strains I do not predicate,
  'Tis that I still retain my "buff and blue";
My politics as yet are all to educate:
  Apostasy's so fashionable, too,
To keep *one* creed's a task grown quite Herculean:
Is it not so, my Tory, Ultra-Julian?

# On This Day I Complete My Thirty-Sixth Year

### 1

'Tis time this heart should be unmoved,
  Since others it hath ceased to move:
Yet, though I cannot be beloved,
    Still let me love!

### 2

My days are in the yellow leaf;
  The flowers and fruits of Love are gone;
The worm, the canker, and the grief
    Are mine alone!

### 3

The fire that on my bosom preys
  Is lone as some Volcanic isle;
No torch is kindled at its blaze—
    A funeral pile.

### 4

The hope, the fear, the zealous care,
  The exalted portion of the pain
And power of love, I cannot share,
    But wear the chain.

### 5

But 'tis not *thus*—and 'tis not *here*—
    Such thoughts should shake my soul, nor *now*,
Where Glory decks the hero's bier,
        Or binds his brow.

### 6

The Sword, the Banner, and the Field,
    Glory and Greece, around me see!
The Spartan, borne upon his shield,
        Was not more free.

### 7

Awake! (not Greece—she *is* awake!)
    Awake, my spirit! Think through *whom*
Thy life-blood tracks its parent lake,
        And then strike home!

### 8

Tread those reviving passions down,
    Unworthy manhood!—unto thee
Indifferent should the smile or frown
        Of Beauty be.

### 9

If thou regret'st thy youth, *why live*?
    The land of honourable death
Is here:—up to the Field, and give
        Away thy breath!

## 10

Seek out—less often sought than found—
  A soldier's grave, for thee the best;
Then look around, and choose thy ground,
    And take thy Rest.

# Remember Thee! Remember Thee!

### 1

Remember thee! remember thee!
  Till Lethe quench Life's burning stream
Remorse and Shame shall cling to thee,
  And haunt thee like a feverish dream!

### 2

Remember thee! Aye, doubt it not.
  Thy husband too shall think of thee:
By neither shalt thou be forgot,
  Thou *false* to him, thou *fiend* to me!

# Epistle To Augusta

### I

My Sister! my sweet Sister! if a name
Dearer and purer were, it should be thine.
Mountains and seas divide us, but I claim
No tears, but tenderness to answer mine:
Go where I will, to me thou art the same—
A loved regret which I would not resign.
There yet are two things in my destiny,—
A world to roam through, and a home with thee.

### II

The first were nothing—had I still the last,
It were the haven of my happiness;
But other claims and other ties thou hast,
And mine is not the wish to make them less.
A strange doom is thy father's son's, and past
Recalling, as it lies beyond redress;
Reversed for him our grandsire's fate of yore,—
He had no rest at sea, nor I on shore.

### III

If my inheritance of storms hath been
In other elements, and on the rocks
Of perils, overlooked or unforeseen,
I have sustained my share of worldly shocks,
The fault was mine; nor do I seek to screen
My errors with defensive paradox;
I have been cunning in mine overthrow,
The careful pilot of my proper woe.

## IV

Mine were my faults, and mine be their reward.
My whole life was a contest, since the day
That gave me being, gave me that which marred
The gift,—a fate, or will, that walked astray;
And I at times have found the struggle hard,
And thought of shaking off my bonds of clay:
But now I fain would for a time survive,
If but to see what next can well arrive.

## V

Kingdoms and Empires in my little day
I have outlived, and yet I am not old;
And when I look on this, the petty spray
Of my own years of trouble, which have rolled
Like a wild bay of breakers, melts away:
Something—I know not what—does still uphold
A spirit of slight patience;—not in vain,
Even for its own sake, do we purchase Pain.

## VI

Perhaps the workings of defiance stir
Within me—or, perhaps, of cold despair,
Brought on when ills habitually recur,—
Perhaps a kinder clime, or purer air,
(For even to this may change of soul refer,
And with light armour we may learn to bear,)
Have taught me a strange quiet, which was not
The chief companion of a calmer lot.

## VII

I feel almost at times as I have felt
In happy childhood; trees, and flowers, and brooks,
Which do remember me of where I dwelt,
Ere my young mind was sacrificed to books,
Come as of yore upon me, and can melt
My heart with recognition of their looks;
And even at moments I could think I see
Some living thing to love—but none like thee.

## VIII

Here are the Alpine landscapes which create
A fund for contemplation;—to admire
Is a brief feeling of a trivial date;
But something worthier do such scenes inspire:
Here to be lonely is not desolate,
For much I view which I could most desire,
And, above all, a Lake I can behold
Lovelier, not dearer, than our own of old.

## IX

Oh that thou wert but with me!—but I grow
The fool of my own wishes, and forget
The solitude which I have vaunted so
Has lost its praise in this but one regret;
There may be others which I less may show;—
I am not of the plaintive mood, and yet
I feel an ebb in my philosophy,
And the tide rising in my altered eye.

## X

I did remind thee of our own dear Lake,
By the old Hall which may be mine no more.
*Leman's* is fair; but think not I forsake
The sweet remembrance of a dearer shore:
Sad havoc Time must with my memory make,
Ere that or thou can fade these eyes before;
Though, like all things which I have loved, they are
Resigned for ever, or divided far.

## XI

The world is all before me; I but ask
Of Nature that with which she will comply—
It is but in her Summer's sun to bask,
To mingle with the quiet of her sky,
To see her gentle face without a mask,
And never gaze on it with apathy.
She was my early friend, and now shall be
My sister—till I look again on thee.

## XII

I can reduce all feelings but this one,—
And that I would not;—for at length I see
Such scenes as those wherein my life begun—
The earliest—even the only paths for me—
Had I but sooner learnt the crowd to shun,
I had been better than I now can be;
The Passions which have torn me would have
        slept—
*I* had not suffered, and *thou* hadst not wept.

## XIII

With false Ambition what had I to do?
Little with Love, and least of all with Fame;
And yet they came unsought, and with me grew,
And made me all which they can make—a Name.
Yet this was not the end I did pursue;
Surely I once beheld a nobler aim.
But all is over—I am one the more
To baffled millions which have gone before.

## XIV

And for the future, this world's future may
From me demand but little of my care:
I have outlived myself by many a day,
Having survived so many things that were;
My years have been no slumber, but the prey
Of ceaseless vigils; for I had the share
Of life which might have filled a century,
Before its fourth in time had passed me by.

## XV

And for the remnant which may be to come
I am content; and for the past I feel
Not thankless,—for within the crowded sum
Of struggles, Happiness at times would steal,
And, for the present, I would not benumb
My feelings farther.—Nor shall I conceal
That with all this I still can look around,
And worship Nature with a thought profound.

## XVI

For thee, my own sweet sister, in thy heart
I know myself secure, as thou in mine;
We were and are—I am, even as thou art—
Beings who ne'er each other can resign;
It is the same, together or apart—
From Life's commencement to its slow decline
We are entwined—let Death come slow or fast,
The tie which bound the first endures the last!

## On the Bust of Helen by Canova

In this belovèd marble view
    Above the works and thoughts of Man,
What Nature *could* but *would not* do,
    And Beauty and Canova *can!*
Beyond Imagination's power,
    Beyond the Bard's defeated art,
With Immortality her dower,
    Behold the *Helen* of the heart.

## Last Words on Greece

What are to me those honours or renown
  Past or to come, a new-born people's cry?
Albeit for such I could despise a crown
  Of aught save laurel, or for such could die.
I am a fool of passion, and a frown
  Of thine to me is as an adder's eye
To the poor bird whose pinion fluttering down
  Wafts unto death the breast it bore so high;
Such is this maddening fascination grown,
  So strong thy magic or so weak am I.